# Sounds Christmas!

## Piano Stylings of Favorite Melodies

## Lynn Freeman Olson

## Contents

# Joy to the World

Joy to the world! The Lord is come: Let earth receive her King;
Let ev'ry heart prepare Him room, And heav'n and nature sing,
And heav'n and nature sing, And heav'n, and heav'n and nature sing.
And heav'n and nature sing, And heav'n and nature sing,
And heav'n and heav'n and nature sing.

Handel
*Arr. by Lynn Freeman Olson*

**Brightly**

# O Come, All Ye Faithful

O come, all ye faithful, joyful and triumphant,
O come ye, O come ye to  Bethlehem;
Come and behold Him, born the King of angels!
O come, let us adore Him, O come, let us adore Him,
O come, let us adore Him, Christ the Lord.

Oakeley, trans.

Reading
*Arr. by Lynn Freeman Olson*

**Moving sturdily**

# It Came Upon the Midnight Clear

It came upon the midnight clear, that glorious song of old,
From angels bending near the earth to touch their harps of gold.
"Peace on the earth, good will to men from heav'n's all-gracious King:"
The world in solemn stillness lay to hear the angels sing.
"Peace on the earth, good will to men from heav'n's all-gracious King:"
The world in solemn stillness lay to hear the angels sing.

Sears

Willis
*Arr. by Lynn Freeman Olson*

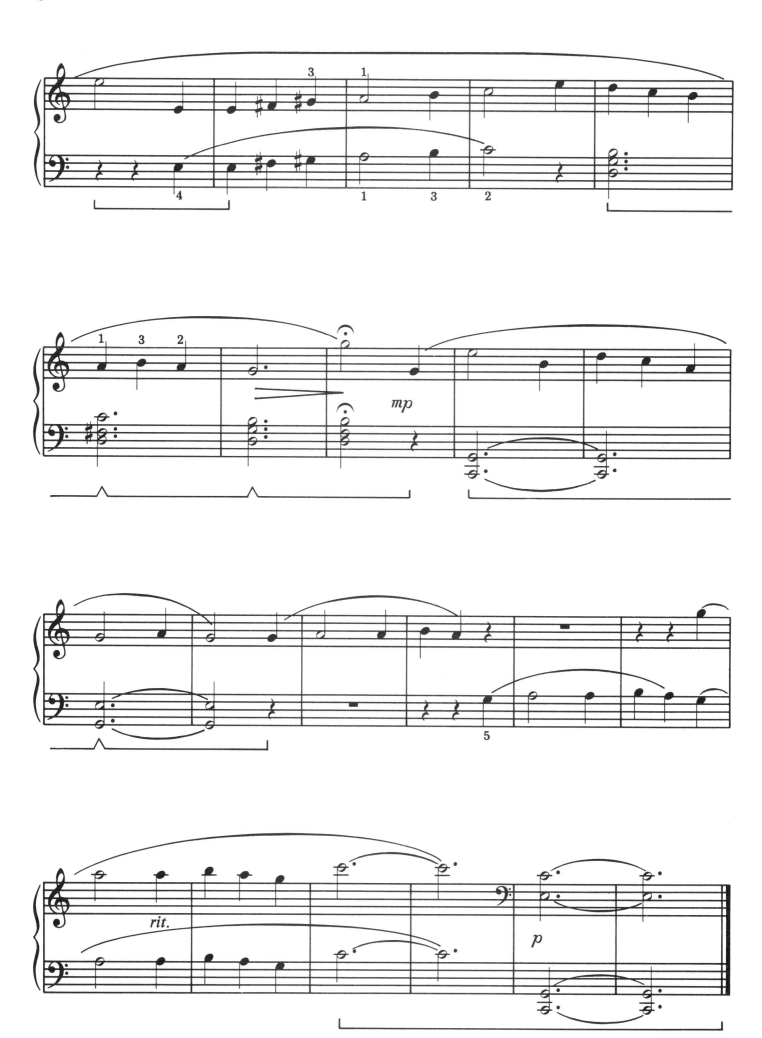

# Silent Night

Silent night! Holy night! All is calm, all is bright
'Round yon virgin Mother and Child. Holy infant so tender and mild,
Sleep in heavenly peace, Sleep in heavenly peace.

Gruber
*Arr. by Lynn Freeman Olson*

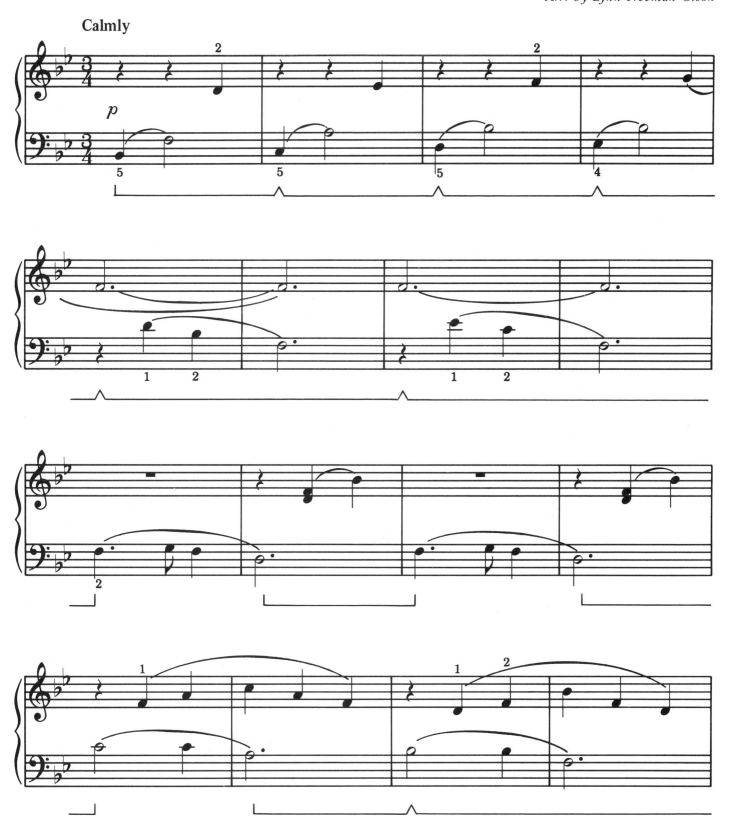

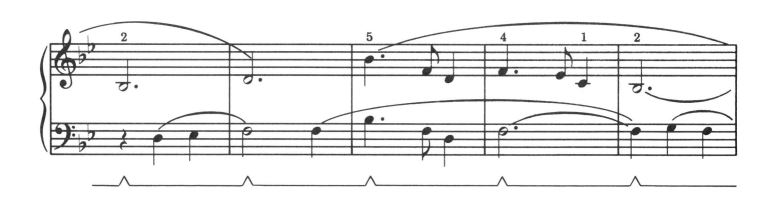

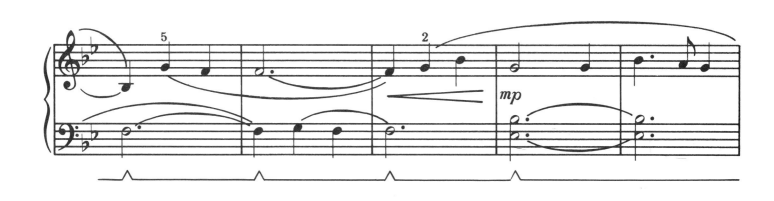

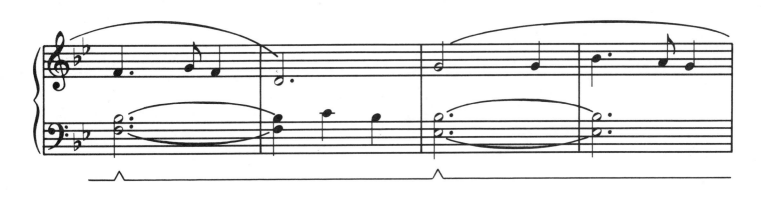
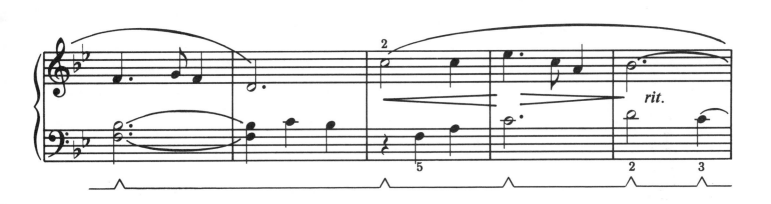

# Angels We Have Heard on High

Angels we have heard on high, Sweetly singing o'er the plains,
And the mountains in reply Echoing their joyous strains.
Gloria in excelsis Deo, Gloria in excelsis Deo.

Chadwick

French
*Arr. by Lynn Freeman Olson*

**Sweetly joyful**

# Hark! The Herald Angels Sing

Hark! the herald angels sing, "Glory to the newborn King!
Peace on earth, and mercy mild; God and sinners reconciled."
Joyful, all ye nations, rise, Join the triumph of the skies;
With angelic hosts proclaim, "Christ is born in Bethlehem."
Hark! the herald angels sing, "Glory to the newborn King!"

Wesley

Mendelssohn
*Arr. by Lynn Freeman Olson*

# The First Noel

The first Noel the angel did say, Was to certain poor shepherds, in fields as they lay;
In fields where they lay keeping their sheep, On a cold winter's night that was so deep;
Noel, Noel, Noel, Noel, Born is the King of Israel.

Traditional
*Arr. by Lynn Freeman Olson*

# Away in a Manger

Away in a manger no crib for a bed,
The little Lord Jesus laid down His sweet head;
The stars in the heavens looked down where He lay,
The little Lord Jesus asleep on the hay.

Luther

German
*Arr. by Lynn Freeman Olson*

# Deck the Hall

Deck the hall with boughs of holly, Fa, la, la, la, la, la, la, la, la,
'Tis the season to be jolly, Fa, la, la, la, la, la, la, la, la,
Don we now our gay apparel, Fa, la, la, la, la, la, la, la, la,
Troll the ancient yuletide carol, Fa, la, la, la, la, la, la, la, la.

Welsh
*Arr. by Lynn Freeman Olson*

**Very brightly**

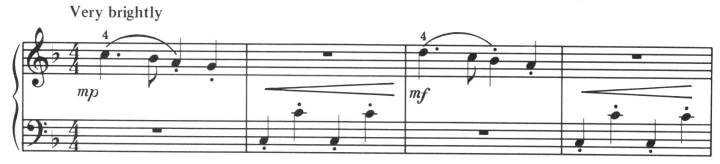

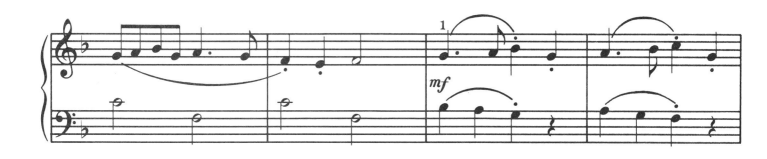

# What Child Is This?

What Child is this Who, laid to rest, on Mary's lap is sleeping?
Whom angels greet with anthems sweet, while shepherds watch are keeping?
This, this is Christ, the King, Whom shepherds guard and angels sing:
Haste, haste to bring Him laud, the Babe, the Son of Mary.

Dix

Old English
*Arr. by Lynn Freeman Olson*

**Moderately**

# O Little Town of Bethlehem

O little town of Bethlehem, How still we see thee lie!
Above thy deep and dreamless sleep, The silent stars go by;
Yet in thy dark streets shineth The everlasting Light;
The hopes and fears of all the years Are met in thee tonight.

Brooks

Redner
*Arr. by Lynn Freeman Olson*

# I Saw Three Ships

I saw three ships come sailing in
On Christmas Day, on Christmas Day;
I saw three ships come sailing in
On Christmas Day in the morning.

Traditional
*Arr. by Lynn Freeman Olson*

**Rolling quickly**

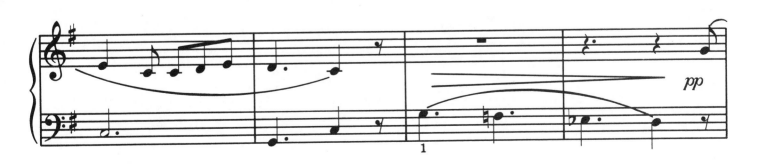

# O Come, Little Children

O come, little children, O come, one and all,
To Bethlehem haste, to the manger so small.
God's Son for a gift has been sent you tonight,
To be your Redeemer, your joy, and delight!

von Schmidt

Schultz
*Arr. by Lynn Freeman Olson*